Cooling Off

Elizabeth Austen

✳ Smithsonian

Consultants

Brian Mandell
Program Specialist
Smithsonian Science Education Center

Chrissy Johnson, M.Ed.
Teacher, Cedar Point Elementary
Prince William County Schools, Virginia

Sara Cooper, M.Ed.
Third Grade Teacher
Fullerton School District

Publishing Credits

Rachelle Cracchiolo, M.S.Ed., *Publisher*
Conni Medina, M.A.Ed., *Editor in Chief*
Diana Kenney, M.A.Ed., NBCT, *Series Developer*
Emily R. Smith, M.A.Ed., *Content Director*
Véronique Bos, *Creative Director*
Robin Erickson, *Art Director*
Michelle Jovin, M.A., *Associate Editor*
Mindy Duits, *Series Designer*
Lee Aucoin, *Senior Graphic Designer*
Smithsonian Science Education Center

Image Credits: p.10 Rosa Irene Betancourt/Alamy; p.17, p.22 NASA; all other images from iStock and/or Shutterstock.

Library of Congress Cataloging-in-Publication Data

Names: Rice, Dona, author. | Smithsonian Institution.
Title: Cooling off / Dona Herweck Rice.
Description: Huntington Beach, CA : Teacher Created Materials, [2020] | "Smithsonian." | Audience: K to grade 3. |
Identifiers: LCCN 2018049784 (print) | LCCN 2018054692 (ebook) | ISBN 9781493868902 (eBook) | ISBN 9781493866502 (pbk.)
Subjects: LCSH: Body temperature--Regulation--Juvenile literature. | Dwellings--Heating and ventilation--Juvenile literature. | Air conditioning--Juvenile literature. | Cold--Juvenile literature. | Heat--Juvenile literature.
Classification: LCC QP135 (ebook) | LCC QP135 .R455 2020 (print) | DDC 612/.01426--dc23
LC record available at https://lccn.loc.gov/2018049784

Teacher Created Materials

5301 Oceanus Drive
Huntington Beach, CA 92649-1030
www.tcmpub.com
ISBN 978-1-4938-6650-2
© 2019 Teacher Created Materials, Inc.
Printed in Malaysia
Thumbprints.21249

Table of Contents

Heating Up

The air is hot. Your clothes stick to your body. It is time to cool off!

A boy drinks cold water after a soccer game.

This dog takes a bath on a hot day.

Ways to Cool Down

What can people do to beat the heat? There are many good tricks for cooling off.

This girl plays with a pinwheel on a hot day.

The wind can cool people off.

Fan It

Waving fans move air. The moving air dries people's sweat. It cools people off. **Electric** fans do the same thing.

This boy cools off in front of an electric fan.

A woman waves a fan to cool down.

No Sweat!

People sweat when they are hot. Moving air **evaporates** the sweat. This cools people down.

Spray It

A **mister** on a hot day can feel good. The light spray of water cools people down.

These kids stand in front of a mister to cool down.

Technology & Engineering

Misting Fan

This is a misting fan. Air and mist work together. They make a person extra cool.

handheld misting fan

Ice It

Nature makes ice. People use it to keep cool. But they should be careful! Ice has to stay cold or it will melt.

This tree is covered in ice.

A boy eats a frozen treat.

Swim It

People can go swimming to cool off. Pools are great for swimming. So are rivers, lakes, and oceans!

This boy swims in a river to cool off.

This boy swims in a pool to cool off.

Wear It

Cooling down is hard in **space**. There is no wind. **Astronauts** wear a special suit. It keeps them cool.

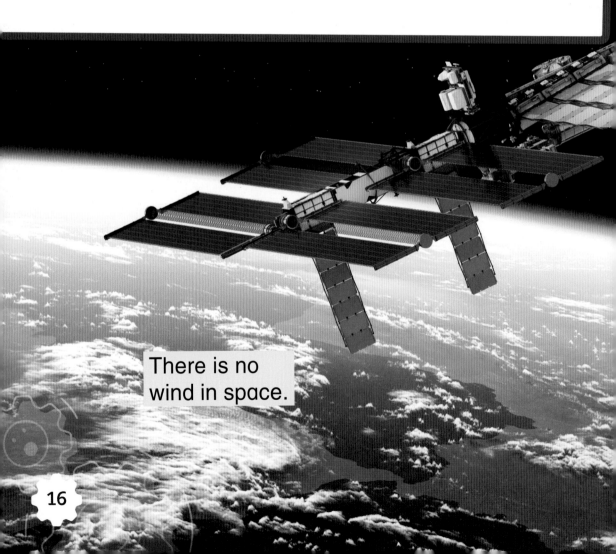

There is no wind in space.

Space Suits

Space suits are white and have tubes. The white color keeps them from getting too warm. The 91 meters (300 feet) of water-filled tubes cool them too.

The Coolest

There are many ways to cool off. Water can do it. Other things can too.

Cooling off can be cool!

Air conditioners are used to keep rooms cool.

Friends cool off in a pool.

STEAM CHALLENGE

The Problem

It is hot! You need to cool off. But you do not have any of the usual things you use to keep cool. You will need to make something to help you cool down.

The Goals

- Your cooling device can be made with any materials you can find.
- Your cooling device must make you feel cooler.
- Your cooling device may not be a simple folded fan.

Research and Brainstorm

Why do people need to keep cool?
What do they use to cool off?

Design and Build

Draw your plan. How will it work?
What materials will you use? Build
your model!

Test and Improve

Try your device. Have a friend try it.
Do they feel cooler? Can you make it
better? Try again.

Reflect and Share

Can your device be used again and
again? Will other people like to use your
device too?

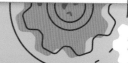

Glossary

astronauts

electric

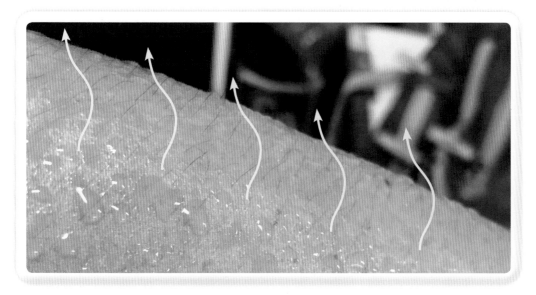

evaporates

mister

space

Career Advice
from Smithsonian

Do you want to design ways to cool people off? Here are some tips to get you started.

"Study history, science, and technology. They will help you learn where we have come from and where we can go!"
— Tim Winkle, Curator

"I study how clothes keep people cool. Read about the history of fabrics. You may be surprised by how many different things you can explore." *— Madelyn Shaw, Curator*